Cheshire Libraries
A 81563766 7

Alex and the Troll

by Clare De Marco and Andy Elkerton

First published in 2011 by
Franklin Watts
338 Euston Road
London
NW1 3BH

Franklin Watts Australia
Level 17/207 Kent Street
Sydney
NSW 2000

A CIP catalogue record for this book is available from the British Library.

ISBN 978 0 7496 9472 2 (hbk)
ISBN 978 0 7496 9478 4 (pbk)

Series Editor: Jackie Hamley
Series Advisor: Catherine Glavina
Series Designer: Peter Scoulding

Printed in China

Franklin Watts is a divison of
Hachette Children's Books,
an Hachette UK company.
www.hachette.co.uk

One day, Alex and his dad built a bridge.

Next morning,
Alex got a surprise.

There was a troll under his bridge!

The troll jumped out. He was big and ugly, and he smelt of rotten cabbages.

"Who's that trip-trapping over my bridge?" growled the troll.

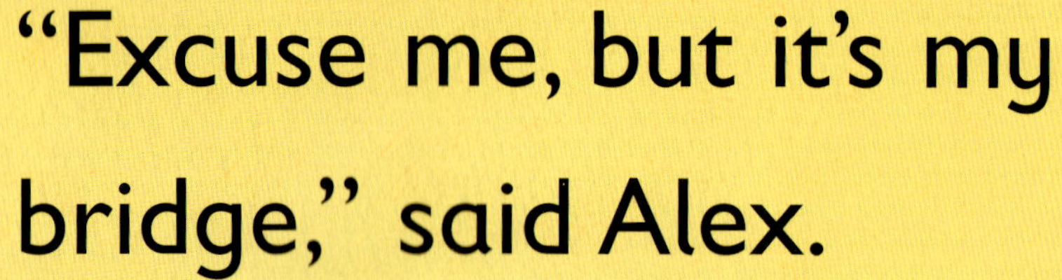

"Excuse me, but it's my bridge," said Alex.

"It's my bridge now!" replied the troll.

"But I built it with my dad,"
said Alex.

"Well I'm not leaving," the troll roared. "It's near the swamp and it smells perfect."

Alex stomped home.
He thought about how
to get rid of the troll.

"The troll likes the bridge because it smells of the swamp," thought Alex.

Alex had an idea. He went into the garden and filled up his wheelbarrow.

Alex tiptoed back to his bridge.

The troll was snoring loudly.

Quietly, Alex put flower pots all over his bridge.

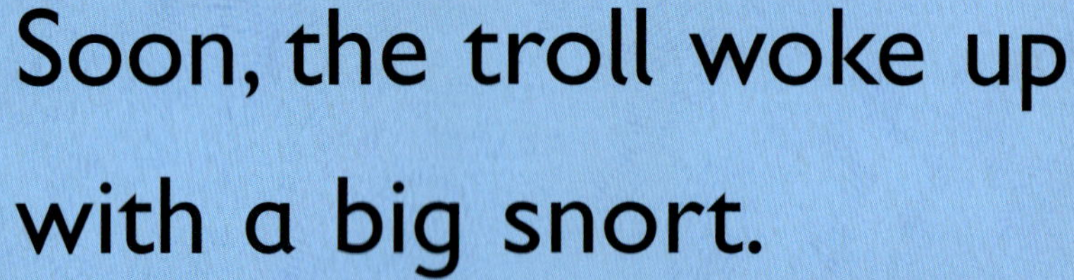

Soon, the troll woke up with a big snort.

"Who's that trip-trapping over my bridge?" he spluttered.

Then the troll started to sneeze.

"Yuck!" he yelled. "It smells disgusting here!"

The troll jumped into the stream and splashed away.

"That got rid of him!"
laughed Alex.

Puzzle 1

Put these pictures in the correct order.
Now tell the story in your own words.
How short can you make the story?

Puzzle 2

annoyed cross
excited

kind mean
smelly

Choose the words which best describe each character. Can you think of any more? Pretend to be one of the characters!

Answers

Puzzle 1

The correct order is:

1d, 2e, 3a, 4f, 5b, 6c

Puzzle 2

Alex The correct words are annoyed, cross.
The incorrect word is excited.

Troll The correct words are mean, smelly.
The incorrect word is kind.

Look out for more Leapfrog stories:

The Little Star
ISBN 978 0 7496 3833 7

Mary and the Fairy
ISBN 978 0 7496 9142 4

Jack's Party
ISBN 978 0 7496 4389 8

Pippa and Poppa
ISBN 978 0 7496 9140 0

The Bossy Cockerel
ISBN 978 0 7496 9141 7

The Best Snowman
ISBN 978 0 7496 9143 1

Big Bad Blob
ISBN 978 0 7496 7092 4*
ISBN 978 0 7496 7796 1

Cara's Breakfast
ISBN 978 0 7496 7797 8

Croc's Tooth
ISBN 978 0 7496 7799 2

The Magic Word
ISBN 978 0 7496 7800 5

Tim's Tent
ISBN 978 0 7496 7801 2

Why Not?
ISBN 978 0 7496 7798 5

Sticky Vickie
ISBN 978 0 7496 7986 6

Handyman Doug
ISBN 978 0 7496 7987 3

Billy and the Wizard
ISBN 978 0 7496 7985 9

Sam's Spots
ISBN 978 0 7496 7984 2

Bill's Baggy Trousers
ISBN 978 0 7496 3829 0

Bill's Bouncy Shoes
ISBN 978 0 7496 7990 3

Bill's Scary Backpack
ISBN 978 0 7496 9458 6*
ISBN 978 0 7496 9468 5

Little Joe's Big Race
ISBN 978 0 7496 3832 0

Little Joe's Balloon Race
ISBN 978 0 7496 7989 7

Little Joe's Boat Race
ISBN 978 0 7496 9457 9*
ISBN 978 0 7496 9467 8

Felix on the Move
ISBN 978 0 7496 4387 4

Felix and the Kitten
ISBN 978 0 7496 7988 0

Felix Takes the Blame
ISBN 978 0 7496 9456 2*
ISBN 978 0 7496 9466 1

The Cheeky Monkey
ISBN 978 0 7496 3830 6

Cheeky Monkey on Holiday
ISBN 978 0 7496 7991 0

Cheeky Monkey's Treasure Hunt
ISBN 978 0 7496 9455 5*
ISBN 978 0 7496 9465 4

For details of all our titles go to: www.franklinwatts.co.uk

*hardback